FAVOURITE
BRITISH
SAUSAGE
RECIPES

Tasty dishes with the great British Banger

Illustrated with
farmyard scenes by
John Frederick Herring

SALMON

Index

Cover: "Barnyard Interior" *Back Cover:* "The Farmyard" *Title page:* "Feeding time"

Printed and Published by J. Salmon Ltd., Sevenoaks, England © Copyright

Sausage and Bacon Pie

A tasty and attractive pie combining bacon and cocktail sausages in a savoury sauce.

PASTRY
6 oz. butter or margarine   12 oz. plain flour   2-3 fl. oz. cold water   Beaten egg, to glaze

FILLING
**12 oz. cocktail sausages   1 tablespoon vegetable oil   1 oz. butter   2 onions, chopped
1 stick celery, finely chopped   1 oz. plain flour   8 fl. oz. milk   3 bacon rashers (chopped)
3 oz. Cheddar cheese, grated   Salt and pepper   2 tablespoons parsley, chopped**

PASTRY: Rub fat and flour together until mixture resembles fine breadcrumbs. Add sufficient cold water to form a firm dough. Cover and chill for 30 minutes.

FILLING: Heat oil in frying pan and fry sausages for 10 minutes. Remove from pan and allow to cool. Melt butter in the pan, add onions, bacon and celery and sauté for 5-6 minutes. Stir in flour and cook for 1 minute. Remove from heat and gradually add milk then return to heat, stirring until sauce thickens and boils. Add cheese, sausages, parsley and seasoning, cover and leave to cool. Preheat oven to 400°F or Mark 6. Grease 9½ inch flan tin. Roll out half pastry and line tin. Add the filling, roll out the remaining pastry and cover the pie. Make 4 vent holes in cover, brush with beaten egg and bake for 30-35 minutes until golden. Serve with vegetables. Serves 4.

Toad-in-the-Hole with Onion Gravy

BATTER
4 oz. flour   ½ level teaspoon salt   **1 egg**   ¼ pint milk   ¼ pint water

1 lb. pork sausages   **4 tablespoons beef dripping**   **2 medium onions, skinned and sliced**
1 tablespoon flour   ½ – ¾ pint beef stock

To prepare the batter, put the flour and salt into a large bowl, make a well and add the egg. Whisk, gradually adding milk and water and drawing in the flour. Beat until smooth. Leave batter to stand for at least 30 minutes. Set oven to 425°F or Mark 7. Put half the dripping into a small roasting pan and place in oven until hot. Place sausages in the hot fat and return to oven for further 5 minutes. Pour batter over the sausages and cook for 40 minutes until well risen and golden brown. While Toad-in-the-Hole is cooking prepare the gravy. Put remaining dripping into a saucepan, add onions and cook gently until soft. Stir in the remaining flour and cook until lightly browned. Remove from heat and gradually add beef stock, stirring well. Return to heat and bring to the boil. Simmer for 10 minutes and serve hot with the Toad-in-the-Hole. Can be served on its own or with seasonal vegetables. Serves 4.

"Farmyard scene"

Pork and Leek Sausages with Black Pudding and Leek Mash

1 lb. pork and leek sausages
2 lbs. potatoes, peeled and cut into chunks
2 leeks, sliced   4 oz. black pudding, cut into cubes
1 eating apple, cored and sliced   ¼ pint cider or apple juice
1 sprig fresh thyme   Milk   Butter

Place potatoes into a saucepan, cover with water and boil for about 12-15 minutes until soft. During the last 8-10 minutes add leeks. Meanwhile, in a small frying pan cook black pudding until golden and crispy. In a large pan dry fry pork and leek sausages for 12-15 minutes, until brown and cooked through. During the last 5 minutes of cooking time add eating apple, skin left on, to the pan and allow to lightly brown. Add cider or apple juice and a sprig of fresh thyme to sausages and allow to bubble until reduced slightly. Drain the potatoes and leeks, and mash with a little milk and a knob of butter. Stir through the black pudding. Serve the sausages with the black pudding and leek mash, apple gravy and seasonal vegetables. Serves 4.

Sausage Lancashire Hotpot

A delicious, warming meal with sage, thyme and black pudding.

**1 lb. chunky pork sausages   2 lbs. potatoes, peeled and thinly sliced
1 tablespoon oil   1 onion, peeled and roughly chopped
½ small butternut squash, peeled and cut into small cubes
4 oz. black pudding, roughly cubed   Fresh sage sprigs
Fresh thyme sprigs   ¼ pint pork stock   Seasoning
1 tablespoon butter   2 oz. Lancashire or Cheddar cheese, crumbled/grated**

Preheat oven to 375°F or Mark 5. Place potatoes in a large pan of cold water and bring to the boil. Cook for a few minutes until the potatoes just begin to soften and drain. Heat oil in large saucepan and brown onion and sausages. Place a layer of potatoes on the base of a large ovenproof casserole dish. Top with sausages, half the butternut squash and black pudding, a sprig of fresh thyme and sage. Add the remaining butternut squash and black pudding and pour over the stock. Top with remaining sliced potato, season, dot with butter and sprinkle with cheese. Cover with foil and cook for 40 minutes, remove foil and cook for a further 30 minutes until browned and golden. Serve with extra steamed seasonal vegetables. Serves 4.

Full English Breakfast

Surely one of the most iconic dishes is the traditional Full English Breakfast which provides an ideal start to the day.

8 oz. lean pork sausages   2 tablespoons oil   2 large eggs
2 large vine tomatoes   2 bacon rashers   2 slices white bread

Cook sausages under grill for 10-12 minutes, turning occasionally, until brown. Slice tomatoes in half and place on grill pan together with bacon rashers to cook for 5 minutes with sausages. While sausages are cooking, using a non-stick frying pan heat oil and cook eggs for 1-2 minutes according to preference. Remove eggs and replace with slices of white bread. Fry until bread lightly browned on both sides, adding more oil if required. Serve fried bread with the eggs, sausages, bacon and tomatoes. Serves 2.

The 'Full English' can be accompanied by a wide variety of other ingredients, some of the most popular being black pudding, mushrooms and baked beans.

Crofter's Casserole

This potato-topped casserole makes an alternative to traditional bangers and mash.

2 tablespoons vegetable oil   8 oz. streaky bacon, diced   1 lb. pork sausages
1 large onion, sliced   1 clove garlic, crushed
1 tablespoon fresh sage, chopped   8 oz. button mushrooms
¾ pint red wine   4 tablespoons tomato purée   ¼ pint chicken stock
1 tablespoon Worcestershire sauce

TOPPING
1 lb. potatoes, peeled and cubed   1 oz. butter
2 oz. grated cheese   Salt and pepper

Preheat oven to 400°F or Mark 6. Heat oil in a large frying pan and fry bacon and sausages for 5 minutes until browned. Add onion, garlic, sage and mushrooms and sauté for further 5 minutes. Add wine to pan and boil for 3 minutes. Add tomato purée, stock and Worcestershire sauce and simmer for 15 minutes. Boil potatoes for about 15 minutes until soft, drain and mash with butter, cheese and seasoning until smooth and creamy. Transfer sausage mixture to large ovenproof dish and spoon or pipe mashed potato around edge. Bake in oven for 20 minutes until potato is golden brown. Serve with seasonal vegetables. Serves 4.

Wiltshire Sausages

An excellent easy meal which, if preferred, can be grilled rather than fried.

1½ lb. lean, boneless pork   ½ lb. shredded suet
½ lb. fresh breadcrumbs   Salt and white pepper
¼ teaspoon ground ginger   ¼ teaspoon mace
¼ teaspoon ground cloves
¼ – ½ teaspoon chopped fresh sage (if desired)
1 egg, beaten   Flour   Fat for frying

Mince the pork, then stir in the suet, breadcrumbs, seasoning and sage (if desired). Combine very well and add sufficient beaten egg to bind the mixture. *Note:* the beaten egg is used to hold the sausage mixture together, as it is not being placed in skins or casings. Mix in ginger, mace and cloves. Form into sausage shapes and coat with a little flour. Heat the fat and fry the sausages until brown. Serve with vegetables. Makes about 10 to 15 sausages.

Oxford Sausages

The recipe for these skinless sausages dates back to the 18th century.

1 lb. lean boneless pork   1 lb. lean boneless English veal
12 oz. shredded suet   8 oz. fresh white breadcrumbs
Grated rind of half a lemon   1 teaspoon ground nutmeg
1 tablespoon chopped mixed fresh parsley, thyme, mint and marjoram
1 teaspoon chopped fresh sage   Salt and black pepper
1 egg, beaten   A little flour for dusting

Mince or very finely chop the pork and veal. Place in a large bowl and add the suet, breadcrumbs, lemon rind, nutmeg and all the herbs. Mix well together and season. Add the egg and stir well until the mixture is well combined and bound together. Flour the hands and form the mixture into sausage shapes. Dust lightly with flour and either cook the sausages under a hot grill, turning frequently until brown and cooked through, or fry in a mixture of oil and butter for about 8 minutes, turning frequently. Serve with creamed potatoes, grilled tomatoes and bacon. Makes approximately 24 sausages.

Pork and Stilton Sausages with Onion Mash

1 lb pork and Stilton sausages
RELISH
1 red onion, peeled and finely sliced   1 clove garlic, finely chopped
1 large red chilli, deseeded and sliced   4 oz. soft brown sugar
5 tablespoons cider or apple juice   1 eating apple, peeled, cored and sliced
3 plums, stoned and quartered   1 pinch ground allspice
MASH
2 lbs. potatoes, peeled and chopped   1 teaspoon vegetable oil
1 large onion, peeled and finely sliced   Knob of butter   Milk

To make relish place red onion, garlic, red chilli, soft brown sugar, cider, apple and plums in a suitable saucepan. Bring to the boil adding the allspice, stirring well throughout. Cover and cook on a reduced heat for about 25 minutes until fruit is soft and liquid reduced to leave syrupy texture. Remove from heat and allow to cool. To make mash place potatoes in saucepan and boil for about 15 minutes until soft. Meanwhile, heat oil in frying pan and fry onion until golden and crispy. Drain the potatoes and mash with butter and a little milk and stir in the onion. Meanwhile, grill sausages for about 12-15 minutes until brown and cooked through. Serves 4.

Bangers and Bows

This tasty sausage and pasta dish makes a substantial mid-week family meal.

1 lb. spicy pork sausages   8 oz. farfalle pasta
1 tablespoon vegetable oil
1 green pepper, deseeded, halved and sliced
1 red pepper, deseeded, halved and sliced
1 medium onion, chopped   1½ oz. butter
1½ oz. plain flour   1 pint milk
4 oz. Cheddar cheese, grated   Salt and pepper
2 tomatoes, sliced   Chopped parsley to garnish

Preheat oven to 375°F or Mark 5. Heat oil in a frying pan and fry sausages until brown. Cut sausages into 1 inch chunks. Place pasta in large pan of boiling water and cook for 10-12 minutes until soft. Meanwhile, remove oil from saucepan and return to heat, adding the onions and peppers and sauté for 3 minutes. Melt butter in a saucepan, add flour and stir until smooth. Remove from heat and stir in half of milk. Return to heat and stir until thick. Add remaining milk, stirring until sauce thickens and boils. Add 3 oz. of the cheese and seasoning. Drain pasta, return to pan and add sausages, vegetables and sauce. Mix well and place in ovenproof dish. Garnish with tomatoes and sprinkle with remaining cheese and cook in oven for 30 minutes. Garnish with parsley and serve. Serves 4.

Curried Sausage Savoury

4 oz. pork sausages   1 large onion, chopped
2 tablespoons oil   4 oz. rice   3-4 teaspoons curry powder
Salt and pepper   ½ pint chicken stock
4 oz. mushrooms, sliced

Heat oil in frying pan and fry sausages and onion until sausages are brown and onion transparent. Add rice, stirring continuously with a wooden spoon, and cook until translucent. Add curry powder (adjust amount to personal taste), season with salt and pepper and add stock. Cover pan and simmer on a low heat for 15 minutes. Add mushrooms and continue to cook until all the liquid is absorbed and rice is soft. Serve with seasonal vegetables. Serves 2.

"Farmyard friends"

Venison Sausages Braised in Red Wine

2 lbs. venison and bacon sausages   1 oz. butter
1 shallot or ½ onion, peeled and chopped
1 clove garlic, peeled and chopped   10 fl. oz. red wine
Bouquet fresh herbs – parsley, thyme, bay leaf, piece celery
Generous pinch of ground allspice   2 teaspoons potato flour
2 tablespoons redcurrant jelly   Salt and freshly milled black pepper
1 tablespoon freshly chopped parsley/chives

Preheat oven to 375°F or Mark 5. Separate sausages. Melt butter in heavy based frying pan. Add shallot or onion and garlic and cook for 2-3 minutes. Add sausages and cook on all sides for 4-5 minutes. Pour red wine into pan, add bouquet of herbs, celery and allspice and bring to the boil. Transfer pan contents to preheated oven dish and cook for 15-20 minutes or until sausages are cooked. Remove herbs and transfer sausages to a hot serving dish. Blend potato flour with tablespoon cold water and stir into oven dish with redcurrant jelly. Stir the sauce until it thickens. Season to taste, pour over sausages and sprinkle chopped parsley or chives on top. Serve with creamed potatoes. Serves 4 to 6.

Mustard Grilled Sausages with Caramelised Apples

1 lb. pork sausages   4 tablespoons oil   1 onion, chopped
1 tablespoon brandy   1 tablespoon flour   1 teaspoon tomato purée
6 tablespoons white wine   ¼ pint stock   4 tablespoons double cream
1 teaspoon green peppercorns   1 teaspoon Dijon mustard
2 eating apples, peeled and cored   1 oz. unsalted butter
1 tablespoon brown sugar   2 tablespoons water

Heat oil in a pan, add the onions and cook over a medium heat until golden. Add the brandy and burn off. Stir in the flour and cook with the purée for 1 minute before pouring in the wine. Add the stock, double cream and bring to the boil. Add the peppercorns and reduce the sauce by half its volume. Meanwhile, brush the sausages all over with the mustard, place on a grill pan, spoon a little remaining oil over each one and grill for 10-12 minutes until thoroughly cooked. Meanwhile, cut each apple into horizontal slices about ½ inch thick or chunky wedges. Heat the butter and sugar in a frying pan, add the apples, water and cook for 2-3 minutes on each side until caramelised. Serve sausages on a bed of chips, coat with peppercorn sauce and top with the caramelised apple slices. Serves 4.

Sausage and Bean Pie

A variation on bangers and mash and shepherds pie.

1½ lbs. potatoes, peeled and chopped   1 lb. pork sausages
1 tablespoon vegetable oil   2 onions, chopped
1 can baked beans   1 teaspoon chilli powder
Salt and pepper   2 tablespoons milk   ½ oz. butter
6 oz. Cheddar cheese – thinly sliced

Preheat oven to 400°F or Mark 6. Boil potatoes until tender. Meanwhile, grill the sausages for 10-12 minutes until browned, turning occasionally. In a frying pan heat the oil, add onions and fry until soft. Cut sausages into thick slices and mix with the beans, chilli powder and seasoning. Put in an ovenproof dish and top with the onions and cheese slices. Drain and mash potatoes with milk and butter, season to taste and spread on top of the dish over cheese and onions. Cook in oven for 20-30 minutes. Serves 4.

Barbeque Sausages

These sausages wrapped in smoked bacon and cheese with a
barbeque sauce are a favourite with children.

1 lb. large pork and beef sausages
8 slices processed cheese
8 rashers smoked back bacon (derinded)

SAUCE
1 tablespoon vegetable oil   1 onion, peeled   1 oz. brown sugar
2 teaspoons English mustard   2 tablespoons Worcestershire sauce
14 oz. tin chopped tomatoes   1 tablespoon parsley, chopped
Salt and pepper

Grill sausages until browned and leave to cool a little. Place cheese slices on
bacon rashers and roll around sausages, one per sausage. Secure with cocktail
sticks and return to grill for approximately 10 minutes, turning occasionally,
until bacon is cooked. To make sauce, heat oil in saucepan, add onions and
sauté until softened.   Stir in the sugar, mustard, Worcestershire sauce,
tomatoes, parsley and seasoning. Bring to the boil and simmer for 5 minutes.
Transfer to a serving bowl and serve with sausages. Serves 4.

Kidney and Sausage Casserole

*This is an old and economical farmhouse recipe. The flavour is improved
if it is made the day before required and reheated.*

1 oz. butter   2 onions, sliced
1 to 2 tablespoons flour, seasoned with a pinch of dry mustard powder
1 lb. pork sausages   2 to 3 lambs' kidneys, wiped, cored and sliced
Bouquet garni of parsley, thyme and sage
Salt and black pepper   1 to 2 pints pork stock
Chopped fresh parsley for garnish

Set oven to 300°F or Mark 2. Melt the butter in a frying pan and lightly fry
the onion until soft, but still transparent, then stir in the seasoned flour. Prick
the sausages lightly with a fork and place in a casserole dish with the kidneys.
Add the bouquet garni of herbs and season. Pour the stock over the onion and
flour mixture in the pan and bring to the boil, stirring, then pour sufficient
into the casserole to cover the contents. Cover and cook for about 5 hours.
Discard the herbs and allow the mixture to cool overnight. Next day, set oven
to 325°F or Mark 3 and cook the casserole for 30 to 40 minutes until
completely heated through, topping up the gravy if necessary. Sprinkle with
chopped parsley and serve with mashed potatoes, carrots and a green
vegetable. Serves 4.

Sausage Cobbler

Use plump butcher's sausages, either plain or herby flavoured, as personal choice.

1 lb. sausages   Oil for frying   2 onions, sliced   4 oz. streaky bacon, diced
1 oz. flour   1 large tin chopped tomatoes   2 tablespoons tomato purée
1 tablespoon Worcestershire sauce   1 tablespoon mushroom ketchup
½ pint beef stock   Salt and black pepper   3 oz. button mushrooms, halved

SCONE TOPPING

8 oz. self-raising flour   1 teaspoon dry mustard powder
Pinch of salt   2 oz. butter, softened
1 teaspoon baking powder   1 egg, beaten   ¼ pint milk

Set oven to 425ºF or Mark 7. Cut the sausages into 2 or 3 sections and fry gently in a pan until browned. Transfer to a dish and keep warm. Fry onions and bacon until soft, add the flour and fry for 1 minute. Add the tomatoes, tomato purée, sauces and stock, season and bring to the boil, stirring. Add mushrooms and sausage pieces, simmer for 15 to 20 minutes, then transfer to an ovenproof dish. Meanwhile, make the scone topping. Sift the flour, salt, baking powder and mustard into a bowl and rub in the butter. Add the egg and stir in sufficient milk to mix to a soft dough. Roll out to ½ inch thickness on a floured surface, cut into small scones with a cutter and arrange, overlapping, around the edge of the sausage mixture in the dish. Bake in oven for about 15 minutes until the scones are risen and golden brown. Serves 4.

"The hay cart"

Cumberland Sausages with Onion Mash and Thyme Gravy

1 lb. Cumberland sausages   2 lbs. potatoes
Milk   1 knob butter   1 bunch spring onions, finely chopped
1 teaspoon oil   1 onion, sliced   2 tablespoons flour
½ pint stock   1 tablespoon fresh thyme leaves

Preheat oven to 450°F or Mark 8.   Put Cumberland sausages in a roasting tin and cook in oven for 15-20 minutes until brown and cooked through.   Peel potatoes and cut into chunks. Place into a pan, cover with water and boil for about 15 minutes until soft. Drain and mash with a splash of milk and a knob of butter. Stir through spring onions.

Gravy: Heat oil and cook onion for 5-10 minutes until lightly golden and soft. Stir in flour then gradually stir in stock. Add fresh thyme leaves, bring to boil and allow to simmer and thicken for 5 minutes. Serve the sausages with the onion mash, and gravy with seasonal vegetables. Serves 4.

Sausage Goulash

Inspired by traditional goulash, this sausage alternative makes a satisfying meal.

**8 oz. pork sausages   2 tablespoons oil
1 onion, chopped   2 teaspoons paprika
2 teaspoons flour   1 large tin of tomatoes
½ pint stock   1 pinch of thyme
Salt and pepper   1 green pepper, deseeded and chopped**

Grill sausages until brown. Heat oil in frying pan and fry onion until transparent. Add the paprika and flour and stir in. Cook for about 1 minute. Add the tomatoes, stock, thyme and season to taste with salt and pepper. Cut sausages into lengths of about 1 inch, add to mixture in frying pan and cook for 15 minutes before adding green pepper. Cook for further 15 minutes. Serve with potatoes or rice and seasonal vegetables. Serves 2.

Sausage Twists

These easy-to-make sausage rolls make excellent hors d'oeuvres.

1 lb. small chipolata sausages   8 oz. puff pastry dough   1 beaten egg

Preheat oven to 450°F or Mark 8. Grill or fry sausages for about 6 minutes until partially cooked. Allow to cool. Roll out pastry until wafer thin. Cut into strips and roll round the sausages. Put on a baking tray. Brush with beaten egg. Bake for 15 minutes towards top of oven. Reduce the heat after 7-8 minutes if necessary. Serve with mustard. Serves approximately 8.

Sausage and Mushroom Rice Ramekins

A version of an old traditional recipe.

4 sausages (sliced)   4 oz. rice
1 onion (finely chopped)
4 large mushrooms (sliced)
6 fl. oz. water   Cherry tomatoes (sliced)
Cheese (grated)

Brown the sausages and sauté the mushrooms in a pan in a little oil. Drain off excess oil and add the rice and onions, stir and cook for a few minutes. Stir in the water and season to taste, cover and cook gently for 15 to 20 minutes until the rice is tender. Place rice mixture into individual buttered ramekins, sprinkle with plenty of grated cheese, add a sliced cherry tomato and brown under the grill. Serve with fingers of chunky toast.

Sausage Pot

*This easy dish is delicious served with a large dollop of sour cream
sprinkled with paprika and some crusty bread.*

**1 lb. pork sausages   2 teaspoons oil
1 leak, sliced   1 eating apple   1 red onion
1 clove of garlic   1 tablespoon tomato purée
1 tablespoon Worcestershire sauce
½ pint orange juice   2 tablespoons paprika
2 tablespoons English mustard**

Preheat oven to 325°F or Mark 3. Slice leek, core apple and cut it into wedges.
Peel the red onion and cut into wedges. Crush garlic clove. Heat oil in a
saucepan and cook sausages until lightly browned. Add the leek, apple, red
onion and garlic clove, together with the tomato purée, Worcestershire sauce,
orange juice, paprika and mustard. Stir well, cover and place in oven to cook
for one hour. Serve with mashed potato and seasonal vegetables. Serves 4.

Lorne Sausage

This traditional Scottish recipe for square sliced sausages is often called Lorne Sausage.

**2 lbs. ground/minced beef   2 lbs. ground pork
3 cups fine breadcrumbs   2 teaspoons pepper
2 teaspoons nutmeg   3 teaspoons coriander
3 teaspoons salt   1 cup of water
2 tablespoons vegetable oil**

The beef and pork should not be too lean or the sausage may be too dry. Mix together by hand the beef and pork with the breadcrumbs. Add pepper, nutmeg, coriander, salt and water until the consistency of paste. Place mixture in an oblong pan about 10″ x 4″ x 3″. The amount of mixture may require two pans. Place in the freezer for a little while until it starts to set. Remove and cut into squares to the thickness you like. In a saucepan heat the oil and fry squares until brown and cooked through. Can be served with salad or vegetables. Serves 4.

Pork and Apple Sausages with Parsnip and Potato Mash

1 lb. pork and apple sausages
2 lbs. potatoes, peeled and cut into chunks
8 oz. parsnips, peeled and cut into chunks
½ pint light beer   2 teaspoons sugar
1 tablespoon gravy granules
Butter   Milk

Place potatoes and parsnips into a saucepan with water and boil for 10-15 minutes until soft. Meanwhile, in a large frying pan dry fry sausages for 12-15 minutes until brown and cooked through. Add light beer and allow to simmer for 2-3 minutes. Add sugar and gravy granules, stirring continuously, and allow to thicken. Drain potatoes and parsnips and mash with knob of butter and a little milk. Serve sausages with the mash and seasonable vegetables. Serves 4.

Sausage Bakewells

Made with Lincolnshire sausages, apple and cheese, these tarts make ideal snacks.

8 oz. Lincolnshire chipolata sausages
1 lb. puff pastry   1 pot chunky apple sauce
1 eating apple, cored and sliced
1 small onion, peeled and thinly sliced
1½ oz. Sage, Derby or Cheddar cheese, grated
1½ oz. breadcrumbs

Preheat oven to 400°F or Mark 6. Squeeze sausages at centre, twist and cut to make each one into two. Roll out pastry and cut into circles to fit muffin tin. Push pastry into a pregreased tin. Add to the base ½ teaspoon apple sauce, top with a small sausage and slice of apple and onion. Mix together cheese and breadcrumbs and sprinkle a spoonful on top of each tart. Bake for about 25 minutes until pastry is 'puffed' and golden and sausage browned and cooked. Serve as a snack with vegetables or mixed salad, or cold in a lunchbox or picnic. Makes about 12 tarts.

Sausage Casserole

Thick, meaty pork sausages from a good butcher are best for this dish.
Try using spicy flavoured sausages for variety.

2 lbs. pork sausages   **1 medium onion, chopped**
2 cloves garlic, chopped   **14 oz. tin of tomatoes, thoroughly chopped**
1 tablespoon tomato purée   **1 teaspoon mixed herbs**
1 teaspoon sugar   **Salt and pepper**
1 dessertspoon cornflour   **½ pint vegetable stock**
2 cups frozen peas   **Oil for frying**

Cut the sausages in half. Heat 1 tablespoon of oil in a large saucepan and fry the sausages slowly, until browned. Remove and set aside. Add another tablespoon of oil and fry the onion and garlic until soft but not brown. Replace the sausages and add the chopped tomatoes, tomato purée, herbs and sugar and stir. Mix the cornflour with a tablespoon of stock in a bowl then stir in the remainder of the stock and mix well. Add to the casserole, stir and season well. Bring to the boil, cover and simmer for 35 to 40 minutes, adding more boiling water if required during cooking. Add the peas 5 minutes before the end of the cooking time. Serves 4 to 6.

Spicy Sausages and Rice

A delicious spicy one-pan version of sausages and mash.

Sausages from local butcher (2 each)
Rice (around 2 oz. per person)
1 large red onion, chopped   1 stick celery (chopped)
1 tin chopped tomatoes   Vegetable stock cube
1 teaspoon curry powder   Water

Brown the sausages in a large pan, then add the onion, rice and celery and cook for a few minutes, stirring all the time. Add the tomatoes, stock cube, curry powder and a little water, cover and cook on a low heat for around 20 minutes, until the rice is tender. Serve with bread and lashings of baked beans.

Devilled Sausages

These sausages and devilled dip make an easy meal with potato wedges or chips.

8 lean pork sausages   8 rashers streaky bacon
1 teaspoon English mustard   4 tablespoons tomato ketchup
1 teaspoon Worcestershire sauce

Preheat oven to 350°F or Mark 4. Spread English mustard over rashers of streaky bacon. Wrap the bacon around sausages, place on a baking tray and cook in oven for 15-20 minutes until cooked through. Meanwhile, mix tomato ketchup with English mustard and Worcestershire sauce to make a devilled dip. Serve with chips or potato wedges. Serves 3 to 4.

Cabbage and Sausage Casserole

A useful, tasty and inexpensive dish for the winter months.

3 rashers streaky bacon, derinded and chopped
1 medium onion, peeled and chopped
½ large cooking apple, peeled, cored and chopped
1-1¼ lb. Savoy cabbage, shredded   Salt and pepper
1 lb. pork sausages   Cooking oil
Small potatoes and parsley butter to garnish

Set oven to 400°F or Mark 6. Fry the bacon in a little oil until the fat begins to flow, then add and fry the onion and then the apple, until softened. Wash and drain the shredded cabbage, add to the frying pan, season and cook for about 5 minutes. Transfer all the mixture to an overproof baking dish. Next fry the sausages in a little more oil for about 3 minutes, so as to start the cooking process, then place them on top of the cabbage mixture. Bake in the oven until the sausages are cooked through. Meanwhile, peel and cook sufficient small potatoes as required and boil until tender. Drain, toss in parsley butter, arrange around the sausages and serve. Serves 4 to 6.

Sausages with Rich Red Onion Gravy

1 lb. sausages   3 tablespoons oil
2 red onions, sliced   ¼ pint red wine or stock
3 tablespoons redcurrant jelly   3 tablespoons fresh thyme
1 tablespoon gravy granules

Using a large heatproof casserole dish add oil and fry sausages for 4-5 minutes until browned. Add the red onions and fry for a further 2-3 minutes. Mix together the red wine or stock, redcurrant jelly and fresh thyme and poor over sausages. Cover and place in oven to cook for 25-30 minutes. Remove sausages and stir in gravy granules to sauce to thicken. Serve with mashed potato. Serves 4.

Sausage Stew

Thick, meaty pork sausages from a good butcher are best for this dish.
Try using spicy flavoured sausages for variety.

2 lbs. pork sausages   2 tablespoons cooking oil
1 medium onion, chopped   2 cloves garlic, chopped
Large tin of tomatoes, roughly chopped
1 tablespoon tomato purée
1 teaspoon mixed herbs   1 teaspoon sugar
1 dessertspoon cornflour   Salt and pepper
½ pt. vegetable stock   2 cups frozen peas

Cut the sausages in half. Heat 1 tablespoon of oil in a large saucepan and fry
the sausages slowly, until browned. Remove and set aside. Add another
tablespoon of oil to the pan and fry the onion and garlic until soft but not
brown. Replace the sausages and add the chopped tomatoes, tomato purée,
herbs and sugar and stir. Mix the cornflour with a tablespoon of stock in a
bowl then stir in the remainder of the stock and mix well. Add to the
saucepan, stir and season well. Bring to the boil, cover and simmer for 35 to
40 minutes, adding more boiling water if required during cooking. Add the
peas 5 minutes before the end of the cooking time. Serves 4 to 6.

Sausage and Potato Supper

4 rashers bacon, chopped   1 lb. chipolata sausages
4 medium potatoes, peeled and sliced   1 large onion
2 oz. butter   2 teaspoons mixed herbs
4 oz. grated cheese   ½ pint milk

Preheat oven to 375°F or Mark 5. Cook sausages and bacon under grill until lightly browned. Cut sausages into slices. Arrange potato slices, onions, bacon and sausages in layers in a greased ovenproof dish, sprinkling each layer with butter, seasoning and herbs. Finish with a layer of potato on top. Cover with grated cheese, pour in milk and bake in oven for about 1 hour until potatoes are soft. Serves 4.

Sausages in Red Wine

1 lb. pork sausages   ½ lb. streaky bacon, cut into cubes
½ lb. small onions   ½ teaspoon dried thyme
1 bayleaf   1 clove garlic, crushed   1 teaspoon flour
½ pint red wine   6 oz. mushrooms, sliced
Lard   2 teaspoons oil   Salt and pepper

Melt lard in ovenproof casserole dish and fry sausages until brown. Remove sausages from casserole and add bacon cubes and onions. Fry until brown. Sprinkle flour over mixture and poor in red wine. Return sausages to casserole and add garlic, bayleaf, thyme and season to taste. Cover and simmer gently for 30 minutes.

Meanwhile, add oil to a frying pan and brown mushrooms. Stir mushrooms into casserole after it has simmered for 30 minutes and cook for a further 20 minutes without lid. Serve with mashed potato. Serves 3.

English Breakfast Risotto

4 sausages   4 rashers bacon
2 vine tomatoes, cut in half
4 oz. grilling mushrooms
1 onion, chopped
4 large eggs, hard boiled and chopped
¼ pint milk   1 tablespoon oil
8 oz. risotto rice
6 tablespoons chicken stock (extra if required)

Grill sausages and bacon until brown and then cut into chunks. Grill mushrooms and tomatoes. In a frying pan add oil and fry onion until transparent, add rice and fry some more, adding milk. Stir until milk is absorbed into rice. Add chicken stock, two tablespoons at a time, wait until nearly absorbed, then add another two tablespoons. Repeat until rice is cooked but still firm. Add chopped sausage, bacon, mushrooms and tomatoes. Stir and cook for 2 minutes. Sprinkle chopped eggs on top. Serves 4.

METRIC CONVERSIONS

The weights, measures and oven temperatures used in the preceding recipes can be easily converted to their metric equivalents. The conversions listed below are only approximate, having been rounded up or down as may be appropriate.

Weights

Avoirdupois	Metric
1 oz.	just under 30 grams
4 oz. (¼ lb.)	app. 115 grams
8 oz. (½ lb.)	app. 230 grams
1 lb.	454 grams

Liquid Measures

Imperial	Metric
1 tablespoon (liquid only)	20 millilitres
1 fl. oz.	app. 30 millilitres
1 gill (¼ pt.)	app. 145 millilitres
½ pt.	app. 285 millilitres
1 pt.	app. 570 millilitres
1 qt.	app. 1.140 litres

Oven Temperatures

	°Fahrenheit	Gas Mark	°Celsius
Slow	300	2	150
	325	3	170
Moderate	350	4	180
	375	5	190
	400	6	200
Hot	425	7	220
	450	8	230
	475	9	240

Flour as specified in these recipes refers to plain flour unless otherwise described.